# Behave Yourself!

*Teaching your children to discipline themselves.*

## Lilly Maytree

Lightsmith Publishers
Thorne Bay, Alaska

Lightsmith Publishers
P.O. Box 19293
Thorne Bay, AK 99919
www.LightsmithPublishers.com

Ordering Information:
Quantity sales. Special discounts are available on quantity purchases by corporations, associations, and others. For details, contact the "Special Sales Department" at the address above. Lightsmith Publishers is an imprint of the Wilderness School Institute, a nonprofit educational organization that offers outdoor youth activities in wilderness settings, including training in wilderness skills and nature studies, as well as the publication of curriculum on related subjects, through the Wilderness School Press, and their children's imprint Summers Island Press.

Behave Yourself!/ Lilly Maytree/ Hardback Edition

ISBN: 978-0-9964953-7-0

*To all those parents who sometimes feel they have no influence over their children at all...yes, you do!*

# CONTENTS

## Introduction

Chapter One
## The Great Controversy

Chapter Two
## The Methods

Chapter Three
## Family Law

Chapter Four
## Changing

Chapter Five
## Phase One

Chapter Six
## Phase Two

Chapter Seven
## Phase Three

Chapter Eight
## Let the House Rule

## Helps

# Introduction

In the hustle of today's working parents with hectic schedules, many families find that their together time is spent mostly trying to maintain order. In the house, at the meals, and especially in those parent/ child relationships. In a society that pushes from every angle for our children to rush headlong toward independence, it is a strange quirk that – compared to other times in history – it has never been so hard to achieve.

Why does a great portion of communication with our children seem to be embroiled with debates over daily chores, bedtime battles that stretch way past story-time, and constant references to boredom? A parent should feel sorry. Or have a little understanding. Or at least realize that "things have changed since you were a kid." Sibling rivalry is the acceptance – not the exception. Right?

The fact is that most parents still possess – deep down inside, somewhere – that wonderful common sense that keeps their world from toppling upside down no matter what it happens to look like from moment to moment. The trouble is we've lost touch with how to apply it. And even if some of us can still remember how Mom or Grandma used to do it, we find ourselves repeating the same phrase as our children: that "things have changed since they were a kid."

And they have.

Back then, they never had to deal with uncensored movies on prime time TV that give you (or your kids) a visual jolt just surfing on through. Or video violence. Or a school system that is often failing in more subjects than it's educating. A person could spend a lot of time proving and getting upset about those things, only it wouldn't be very worthwhile. Because the truth is, everybody's right. You, your parents, and even your kids. There have always been differences between the generations, even in the "good old days." And to be focused on these differences is actually a hindrance to good parenting that keeps us from that most wonderful of Life's secrets that makes all the difference...

Tmes change, people don't.

Unlock the secrets to human nature and you can successfully deal with any child, no matter what age they are. With a few basic rules that are simple to apply, you can start seeing results today, and tomorrow, and any other time you want to "turn the key." And before you say, "But you don't know my kids," you can be sure that – unless you have given birth to alligators instead of children – these things will work for you.

In the following pages we will deal with some common problems of managing behavior in today's homes and how you can teach your children to discipline themselves. That is really the end result we are all looking for. But changing behavior begins first with the ability to deal effectively with your children. So, if while reading the following pages you sometimes feel the spotlight is occasionally turned on you instead of your child... you're right. The truth is there is no greater influence over a child than a parent. That truth is at the very heart of all parent/child relationships. Why?

Because that's human nature.

# THE WHY

> *The clearest method of instruction
> is always the most efficient.*

## Chapter One
## **The Great Controversy**

Most parents will use the same method of discipline with their children that their own parents used with them, whether it was good or bad. There has been great controversy about the effectiveness—and sometimes even the morality—of the various methods. Some of those methods our society has actually stepped into homes and schools to regulate. To spank, or not to spank? It's a decision that involves many elements and careful contemplation of not only the parent's perspective, but the child's.

There is no debate over the fact that children need to be corrected; some more frequently than others. Parents will also generally agree that what works well for one of their children will not always have the same effect on another. But no matter what method you choose, **consistency** and **follow-through** are the two most important ingredients to insure success.

If Jenny gets a spanking for running into the street one time, it should be the same if it happens again. Similarly, if you threaten a spanking if she does, you better follow through and deliver should she decide to put your words to the test. It is the nature of children to test limits, but it is also the nature of children to accept those limits if they are clearly defined. Consistency and follow-through not only saves on frustrations and confrontations in the long run, it provides the benefit of a sense of security for the child as well. Though it may take more time and effort in the beginning, it actually becomes easier later on. Is it worth the time to make this "investment of discipline" in the long run? You bet it is. Because no matter how you decide to deal with it, parenting is for the long run, anyway.

The clearest method of instruction is always the most efficient, no matter how complicated or simple it is. The three most popular methods of discipline are **time out**, **restriction of privileges**, and **spanking**. Let's take a closer look at each of these, and the benefits or drawbacks they present.

## TIME OUT

This is the most effective method of correction for younger children for the following reasons. It is immediate, it is uncomfortable, and it gets quick results. The difficulties that "time outs" sometimes impose are usually with a child's inability to handle inactivity (especially for those with hyperactive disorders), and the occasional circumstance where there is no place to remove the child from the current activity in order to carry it out.

## RESTRICTION OF PRIVILEGES

Restriction of privileges works better for older rather than younger children for the simple reason that the consequences of the misconduct are delayed. A younger child who has to wait until tomorrow or next week to forfeit a favorite activity must be old enough to know how far away next week is, or at least able to remember a misbehavior from one day to the next. If there is not sufficient recall to contemplate or anticipate the cost, the method loses impact.

However, restriction of privileges does give children the lesson of personally having to pay for their own mistakes. The drawback to this method is the propensity for parents to withdraw things that are not relative to the "crime" without taking enough thought as to the after-effects on their children. It is also common to use this correction device too frequently. Sadly, there are many children that spend the greater portion of their free time perpetually "grounded."

## SPANKING

If you are a parent with a tendency to display anger when correcting your child — much less if you have an anger problem in general — you should not resort to spanking. It's true that this form of correction gets the most immediate results but it has some dangerous pitfalls to watch out for.

While it is beneficial to show disapproval toward certain behaviors, it is never beneficial to show anger toward your child as a person. This kind of negative feedback almost always produces feelings of inadequacy and low self-esteem later on. It is also true that improper forms of physical correction (such as unexpected smacks, overly hard ones, or such punishments for inconsistent reasons) shows disrespect to a child as a human being. Unfairness causes some of the deepest wounds in children and has much the same result an adult would have toward an employer that was illegally docking his pay.

To inflict physical discomfort for any reason can only work if it is justified. Without this, it will produce a similar effect to blowing an electric fuse: any power and light that was desired in the first place (which should be the aim of all forms of discipline) is reduced to a confusion of darkness and chaos until the proper "circuits" are restored.

There are parents that have achieved high levels of good behavior in their children without ever having spanked them. At the same time, there are parents that consistently spank who have consistently ill-behaved kids. The secret to any method of discipline is to find the right method for the individual. That's because discipline is a relationship, not a philosophy. The best forms of discipline are the ones that promote mutual love and respect between parent and child.

Following is a checklist to measure the accuracy of disciplinary methods, to help you decide if you should "readjust" some of yours, or maybe even change them completely.

## ✔ CHECKLIST

- ✔ What are the results? Do your corrections sufficiently cut down or get rid of the undesired behavior?

- ✔ How do you feel afterward? Do you have frequent regrets for being too harsh with your child? Do you ever over-indulge them in other ways to make up for it?

- ✔ Do you consistently struggle with the same unwanted behaviors in spite of frequent discipline?

- ✔ Does your child frequently lie or avoid you instead of following rules?

- ✔ Is your child disrespectful toward you?

- ✔ Do you ever feel resentment for having to deal with your children's inappropriate behaviors?

- ✔ If you had extra time would you rather be alone instead of doing something with your children?

- ✔ Do your children more frequently exasperate or embarrass you rather than make you proud?

If you are not happy with your answers to two or more of these questions, your current method of discipline needs some adjusting. If you are unhappy or dissatisfied with most of them, then you need to try something different. Whatever you do, don't give in to the temptation to feel disappointed at having to change or make changes.

Instead, be encouraged that you are sensitive and dedicated enough to being a successful parent to realize the need. Most parents never do. Which is a sad statistic considering that children are the most forgiving and resilient members of the human race.

What's more, the effects of experiencing forgiveness and resiliency have far-reaching benefits to the development of human character. Finding a method of discipline that works for both you and your child is good parenting.

And good parenting makes life good.

> *Start with the child's own thinking processess.*

## Chapter Two
## **The Methods**

Considering the number of personality types there are within the human race it is no wonder that a method of discipline that works well for one child will not always work for another. Parents continually marvel that children born of the same family can be so different from each other. There are also a great number of families that are made up of a mixture of "yours, mine, and ours," and we should not be surprised that the parenting process has taken on new complexities.

It is not uncommon to have within the same family a child that will persist in bad behavior no matter how many spankings he gets and another that will crumble and never do the thing again, when you simply cast a "firm eye" in her direction. The answer to this mystery is for the parent to discern the differences in each child, and adjust the methods accordingly. Which takes time. And awareness. Both of which can only come about by accurate observation of how your children react to various situations.

It takes a closer look than to simply notice that your children fight about something every night when you are right in the middle of making dinner. Is it your routine to yell,

"Knock it off!" from the kitchen and go on with your preparations, only to face the same fiasco tomorrow? Many parents do. Or, maybe they actually succeed in dragging you away from the chore to be the grand moderator of their dispute.

However you choose to deal with the problem, the secret to success in this situation is to realize that the nightly arguing is not the real problem. The real problem is attention. For some reason, your children feel they are not getting enough from you, whether their observation is accurate, or not. It might be comforting to point out that much of the time this observation is not accurate. But that doesn't make it any less of a problem.

The answer? Give them more attention. But before you say, "How in the world can I do that, when I have to keep up with a full time job, the meals, the house..." let's take a closer look at what attention really is. Attention is respect. That doesn't mean you have to stop your dinner preparations in order to give in to their desire to control your time. At the same time, it doesn't mean that you should use the perpetual ignoring routine on them, either.

Knowing your children well enough and taking the time to find out the best way to deal with their particular personalities is having respect for them as individuals. No matter how old they are. And that is the kind of attention they are really after.

Do you have a child that is constantly "needling" the others? Do you have one that can't sit still long enough to let you get anything done? Or maybe you have a child that spends so much time in his room with video games that you're lucky you can even get him to come to dinner. Each of these is a different symptom of the same problem: a lack of attention. Let's fix the attention problem by looking at each of these types of children in a different way.

## THE NEEDLER

This type of child is a very social person who– when they can't get positive feedback from people– will settle for negative feedback simply to maintain interaction. This is a child who needs to be constantly participating in something. They need frequent—if not constant—recognition. The solution? More responsibility. This kind of a child makes a wonderful helper and thrives on the satisfaction of not only mastering new tasks, but in doing things for others.

This child will not respond well to either a time out method of discipline, or even spanking. The quickest and most beneficial discipline for the "needler" is to get an immediate consequence for those behaviors that incorporates their full attention and energy. They need a chore. To have him set the table, make the salad, or unload the dishwasher, not only removes him from the group temporarily, it gives him something to do. Which was what he needed in the first place.

It also allows him to pay for his infraction in an acceptable manner while still maintaining some semblance of personal respect. What's more, if you will take the opportunity to praise him for doing a good job rather than responding, "… and you'll get another one if you bother anybody, again!" you'll even get a change in attitude. Which is an all-time big deal on any parent's list.

## THE HYPERACTIVE

In the same way that the "needler" needs something to do, the hyperactive child needs something to do, too, but for different reasons. This kind of child is driven more by physical energy than social need. While he may not bother others during a group television time, he might quietly (and often thoughtlessly) pull the stuffing out of a hole in the upholstery while watching. In the early years, this type of child tends to be the climber or explorer variety. They often send parents to their wits end having to deal with some of the situations they get into. Later on (and especially if they have a teacher that is not adept at handling this kind of behavior), they are often in frequent trouble at school.

Once again, time out and spanking are merely opportunities for the escalation of bad behaviors for these types of children. And once again, they need to be doing something. But unlike the child that merely needs social approval, the hyperactive child needs to be at the edge of physical endurance most of the time. The consequence of a chore needs to be more physical for them, such as taking out the trash (which constitutes a trip outside), carrying laundry, or scrubbing pots and pans.

This child thrives not so much on approval as being needed. Praise for a difficult achievement is more important to them than a job well done. A change of attitude comes for these children not from approval but from a sudden need that only they can fulfill. A wise parent will take notice when their hyperactive child is on the verge of "erring" and come up with a "sudden need" beforehand.

## THE WITHDRAWN

This type of child lives in "a world of their own." They are not driven by either social or physical desires but rather take solace in their own active imaginations. They are mentally ahead of most children, yet, they often fall into the category of what educators call "mentally lazy." Which is a highly inadequate term. The fact is, these children are not lazy, they are bored. If they neglect mundane schoolwork or a parent's urgent call, it is only because they are actively–and mentally--engaged in more thrilling things. This type of child needs to be inspired and challenged.

"Time out" is the most effective method of discipline for the "withdrawn" child, simply because the experience of being removed from an engaging pastime is almost unbearable for them. As they grow older, the restriction of privileges serves the same purpose. But there is a note of warning here; these types of children are easily offended. And too many offenses can lead to deep resentments. The attitudes of the withdrawn child are well guarded, and often mistaken for being stubborn or hard-headed, when it is really that most wonderful attribute of determination, bound up under lock and key.

All children need dicipline, not only to learn the rules and be kept under control, but to feel secure. They need authority. But authority does not mean who can yell the loudest and have the last word. Or being the one who can physically force them to do something. True authority wears the cap of wisdom.

There are a lot of children in our society who are smarter

than their parents in many ways. Surprisingly, it makes little difference when it comes to parenting because intelligence is not interchangeable with authority. Authority is something we are placed into as opposed to earning. And as history proves, it is often the office of authority that causes a ruler to grow, rather than the road to getting there. The same is true with parenting.

It is the nature of children to be very forgiving and resilient individuals. And as we've said before, their abilities to have faith and trust in the individuals who care for them sometimes surpasses the capacity of adults when put to similar tests. That's a wonderful thing. Nature allows us to "grow up together" with our children, by starting things off with the simplest of interactions: the provision of food, shelter, and handling. By the time they're old enough to judge you, you've had more than enough time to figure things out.

Nevertheless, discipline—of any kind—is often so uncomfortable for parent and child that it is put off as a very last resort. Some families even ignore the issue completely, believing that "out of sight" is truly "out of mind." Which usually refers to the child's mind, not the parent's. Because few children who have no rules, at all, rarely take it upon themselves to go by any.

Following are a few pointers on discipline to help those parents whose methods are doing a better job of wearing them out, rather than of keeping their children in line:

# ✔ CHECKLIST

✔ Any form of discipline should have a positive outcome. If the majority of your confrontations with your children end with being more upset with each other than when you started out… it's time to make some changes.

✔ If you are not seeing any changes in unwanted behaviors after consistently applying efforts in that area, don't be afraid to try something else.

✔ Don't worry about "being fair" in the eyes of other siblings. If Sarah gets a spanking for doing something, and her sister merely gets sent to her room for the same infraction two days later, point out the outcome of the methods instead of the methods themselves. A simple response of, "Wouldn't it be nice if that's all it took for you to behave, too?" is enough to make your point.

✔ Don't hold grudges. When an incident is over–and paid for– it's over. Never give your children the "silent treatment" for hours or days on end, or remind them of all their infractions long afterward. This makes for low self-esteem, and sometimes even feelings of rejection that can take years to mend… if ever.

✔ Let your word be your bond . If you say it, do it. When your children know where your "bottom line" is, they will stop trying to find it.

✔ Listen to your instincts. Don't be in a hurry to take the

advice of others if you "don't feel quite right" about doing it. Parents really do have a built-in sense of what's best for their own children, and sometimes an outsider only sees "the tip of the iceberg" when it comes to the real reasons for your child's behavior.

✔ Always end on a positive note. Make sure things get back to normal between you and your child as quickly as possible after a confrontation. Never let them go to bed or off to school with feelings of resentment or guilt. Reassure them that you love them–no matter what–and only want what's best for them. And insist on a similar response from them.

   If negative feelings linger between you, there is still something to be worked out. It is as important for them not to hold grudges as it is for you. Simply because the quality of their future is at stake.

Discipline is like electricity; there is both a negative and a positive charge. As with all forces of nature, the secret to getting any benefit from it, is in how well you can control it. One of the great fallacies in today's homes is that discipline and authority have to be accompanied by a display of anger in order to carry any weight. This is not true. Anger is a negative thing that produces negative results. Remember: when choosing between negative and positive, positive is always better.

There are many wonderful books on the market these days that offer step-by-step instructions on positive discipline and most of them will do the job. The bottom line in choosing is to decide if it will have positive results for you and your family.

Why is it so important to be positive? Because it's like the difference between light and dark: children will naturally gravitate toward the light.

It's human nature.

## Chapter Three
## **Family Law**

Everyone needs the law: those who break it, those of us who don't, and those who make a living by explaining the differences between these two groups. A person does not have to understand or even know the law to be subject to it. But there is no doubt that a clear understanding of these things makes for a more secure — and more responsible — citizen. The same is true within families.

Families are an individual's first experience with group behavior. And it should be every family's goal to raise individuals who will be self-disciplined enough to never have to brush up against that longer — and often unyielding — arm of our society's laws. Being "brought to task" as an adult has far reaching effects that are sometimes impossible to get out from under. That's why it is vital in early years to develop the respect and discipline it takes to "correct ourselves" before we get there.

"Law awareness" is not something parents have to purposefully set out to cover in their list of "Goals I would like to Accomplish in Raising My Children." It is something they do naturally. A person's attitudes and methods in dealing with the law will be conveyed to their children, simply because children will take on their attitudes and methods of dealing with things. That old saying "Do as I say and not as I do," does not work. Though it might bring a few moments of peace during a fleeting argument (only because you are bigger than them), it is faithfully creating a piece of yourself within their character even as you speak. Children will always do as you do before they do as you say. That's human nature. And this is something that can work for them, or against them, in life.

Every family has laws, whether they have put a name to them or not. And every family spends whatever time it takes to enforce these. The differences lie in how you choose to do it. There is no doubt that some methods are more successful than others. It is not unusual to walk through a public place these days and see a full-blown issue being tried out in family court, no matter who happens to be passing by. You do not have to stay longer than fifteen minutes in the toy department of any store to prove this. And even if you have your darlings trained up well enough not to crumble under these temptations, there are two other children to every one of yours that don't.

That's because humans have a driving force to voice and debate their opinions and it starts at a very early age. Children could spend most of their time doing this if you would let them, but as an adult, there are a few other things that demand your attention, now and again, besides your kids. Getting caught up in situations like this can also be pretty embarrassing.

So what do you do with this fiery little piece of humanity you're forced to deal with day in and day out? Do your best to keep things under control and hope by the time they reach voting age they have developed some sort of wisdom—or at least a little common sense —through the process of osmosis? Possibly. And there are a lot of young adults released out into the world with only "some sort of wisdom, or a little common sense" to get by on. Invariably it makes for unnecessary troubles in the adult world that would have been much easier to learn in the less threatening environment of the home they just came out of.

But if Wisdom and Common Sense are two of the most important things you can give a child, just how do you go about giving it to them? The secret is to look at yourself.

How much advise have you ever taken from others?

Probably not much compared to what you have learned through your own experiences. A lot goes in to the willingness to trust someone else's opinions rather than your own. Nine times out of ten it is a relationship thing, and not so much what someone says but who they are that makes the difference. Which is as it should be. That's human nature. And children are no different. Wonderful things can come from learning from your mistakes, but–like a shotgun– it can also cause some damage when things misfire. If fired at too close a range, it can literally blow the situation to pieces.

The best and most proven method of dealing with these situations is one that goes back thousands of years. It's called the family conference, and it goes as far back through humanity as you would care to trace it. It's hung around this long because it works. Here are some characteristics that differentiate the family conference from other types of family gatherings:

The whole family is involved.

Every member has a vote.

Every member has a right to be heard without being criticized.

All problems are aired and settled by majority rule.

In order to participate, **RULES OF CONDUCT** must be strictly adhered to.

The family conference is one more great way to turn your family time into "prime time" simply because it sets a specific time to deal with things you deal with anyway. The difference is, it channels the "line of fire" to go off at appropriate targets instead of the isles of department stores where someone could sustain injuries.

A child standing in a department store that wants to know exactly why he can't have an official fire-breathing, missile shooting, electronic version of some character of the latest hit-movie might take the answer "Because it costs too much money!" as a personal insult. Like maybe he's not worth that much money — or worse — that he is worth less than the price of a mere toy. Even if you would be the first to insist this isn't true (no matter what mood you're in), he probably won't even bring it up as an argument.

Because the clock is running. He only has a certain amount of time to win or lose this thing and he's going to take his best shot. Which is the hope that you would rather get the thing than argue about it, and work the details out later. How many times has that worked for him?

At least once, or he wouldn't be going for it, again.

The family conference is a non-threatening environment for settling these kinds of disputes without squashing hope and self-esteem to do it. That doesn't mean you whip out your copy of *Robert's Rules of Order* and hold a family conference right there in the middle of the store.

You simply make a little adjustment in the way you respond to the situation. A response of "What a toy! I can see why you would really want one of these. But it's pretty expensive, isn't it? To spend this much money we'd have to talk about it, first, at Family Conference. Maybe you should bring it up, tonight." Which does three important things. It defers the decision until later, the child still has the hope that he might actually get one, and he also has something important to contribute to the group around the conference table.

You mean you really might actually have to buy this thing? Not necessarily. But if it's that important to him, you may have to set up a way that he could earn it (through behavior, chores, allowance, etc.), and then follow through with the plan. But you would be surprised how many of these episodes are no more than passing fancies which — when placed with a value of actual time, effort, or money to get — are not worth it even in the child's eyes. Something that puts the decision-making experience back in his corner. That's the only place it's going to do him any good.

The family conference allows you to pour all your "spur of

the moment" problems into a time slot that you are best equipped to deal with it in. Experience shows that people deal a lot better with things they are prepared for than things they aren't. Even though the family conference has the characteristics mentioned above, it is something that you can successfully mold to your own family's routine to get the fullest benefit from.

If you are a young family, and spend significant time during each day settling disputes and maintaining control, you might need to have one every evening. If you have older children whose problems or concerns tend to come up mostly if they want to do or get something, your conferences can be more occasional. Ultimately the habit of having family conferences will carry over even into the adult years, when it is still the desire of the grown children to seek counsel from their parents, and each other, to help face life's many challenges.

Seeking out the counsel of others is one of the best ways of avoiding some of the mistakes so many of us have had to deal with on our own, and it is a habit that can be cultivated in childhood. How wonderful would it be if one mature family member could still learn from another the hazards of owing thousands of dollars to credit agencies without personally having to go through the unpleasant experience themselves. It is not so hard if they have grown up learning to be honest enough to share things with each other.

However you choose to schedule your family conferences, here are some of the basic rules that will make each conference time more beneficial to everyone:

# ✔ CHECKLIST

✔ Every family member's opinion is important. Schedule family conferences so that all family members can be present to participate. Unless Dad and big brother are off fighting the third world war, this isn't impossible and should be a priority.

✔ Open a complaint department. If you have young children who find it difficult to wait until the rest of the family comes home to settle something, let them write (or you write for them) out a complaint and put it in a box. Assure them that these things will be discussed first at the Family Conference, and they will feel the security of something "tangible" to prove this.

✔ Let the majority rule when it comes to deciding consequences for certain behaviors or establishing new rules for things. You will find the group amazingly fair because they know the same power could be wielded against them next time. This is a good example of a "mini-democracy."

✔ Don't have family conferences during meal times. Matters brought to the conference table can often be emotional and probing, and should never impose on the comfort and security of meal times.

✔ Do not interrupt. Everyone will get a chance to be heard and it is not acceptable to talk when someone else is voicing an opinion.

✔ Say three nice things first, about someone you have a complaint about. This offsets negative criticisms by positive remarks and guards against attitudes that can undermine relationships. If a person cannot do this, then he is being too selfish or narrow-minded about the situation and is not ready to bring that complaint before the group with a reasonable attitude toward working things out. A case in which the issue would have to be deferred for discussion until that time.

Putting family conferences into effect in your home will strengthen your security level. Children will begin to trust that their important issues will be dealt with fairly, and they will feel empowered because they are a necessary ingredient to the process. They will put more thought into their opinions simply because they appreciate that their opinions matter.

Often they will amaze you with their ability to shoulder their part of "family law." They will become adept at negotiating and listening to others, and they will learn that putting fairness into practice benefits everyone. That's when you've opened your door to **Wisdom** and **Common Sense**. And when these two start showing up at your family conference table…

Then you've made it.

> *Behavior effects the quality of life.*

## Chapter Four
# **Changing**

Changing behavior is a necessary part of parenting, especially in this modern era when so much of a child's time is spent with other people. In the old days, our worlds were smaller. It wasn't as difficult to notice if a child "got up on the wrong side of the bed," or to correct some minor infraction that was taking place under a parent's eye. But in this day and age, parents are most likely to have their eyes somewhere else unless there's a problem.

It is also true that teachers and daycare workers are reluctant to point out every little infraction, simply because it is more reasonable (for everybody involved) to take care of discipline themselves unless a problem persists. By that time the unwanted behavior is fairly well ingrained in the child's habits and takes more than a "talking to" to get rid of. If ever. Another ingredient to this dilemma is a parent's avoidance of confrontations in the already limited span of time allotted to spend with their children.

Morning and bedtime routines, by their very nature, are usually consistent enough to produce a false sense of well-being for the mere fact that the activities and participants are the same every day. These brief periods do not allow parents to observe how their child responds to an authority other than themselves, or how they interact with others. All too often, it is an unscheduled parent conference or a dreaded "N" (needs improvement) on a report card that gives an unsuspecting parent the first clue that their little darling has been carrying out an unacceptable behavior for months.

Sadly, what usually ensues is a bitter cycle of "groundings" and similar punishments that tend to increase at an alarming rate instead of producing the desired outcome. This in turn brings about frustrations on both sides that often lead to resentments and bitter disputes in what was once a fairly peaceful home. On top of that, our current trend to relegate every outlandish behavior to a "normal" quest for independence on the child's part sometimes tempts parents not to deal with the issue at all, but to hope instead that it is simply a phase they will one day grow out of.

If Sally does not share her toys in preschool, there is every possibility that the problem will slip by until she is fourteen, when she shocks her parents by being attracted to "the wrong crowd." Why? Because sharing is a respect issue, and as time goes by it is human nature to fall into categories with only those who are similar to yourself. Which has a huge effect on self-image. By the time Mom and Dad finally notice, she has a low self-image (hanging with the wrong crowds) they tend to have difficulty understanding how it could have happened when they always gave her everything she wanted

On the other hand, if Billy is a biter, this will get immediate attention by everybody and the unwanted behavior will be squashed like an intruding insect. This is proven by the simple fact that the only biters to be found in the adult world are vampires.

Which is a different problem, altogether.

Behavior effects the quality of life. Good behavior makes life simple. The child who learns this early will be ahead of the child who doesn't.

The more parents can help their children learn good behaviors, the easier their adjustments and understanding will be in the great wide world ahead of them. Which is why it becomes necessary at sometime or another to change a child's behavior. There are many methods for changing unwanted behaviors, but the one we will be looking at here is geared to implementing the natural impulses of human nature. That's because utilizing drives that are already in motion simply makes the job easier.

Which makes life easier for everybody,

# THE HOW

> *All children need discipline to feel secure.*

Chapter Five
# Phase One

The first step to changing any behavior is to start small. If Johnny is having trouble paying attention at school, the first thing he needs is a reason to change. Other than an irate parent telling him to "Straighten up when the teacher's talking, do you hear me? I don't want to get a note like this, again!"

Equally doomed is a response like, "If you can go all week without getting in trouble, I'll…" A week is huge. It isn't even today; it's floating off somewhere in the future. Between now and a week there are a thousand tantalizing temptations to avoid. Like sitting next to a best friend, or discovering a hangnail, or, the biggest temptation of all… someone else talks to him first.

The world outside of one's home is a very exciting and distracting place. Our public schools have become boring by comparison. The only thing that comes close to weighing in as an equal is a reward. At this point, mere praise from an appreciative parent is not enough. Nor is the promise of a treat or something special at the end of the day if he makes it through all the way without failing his mission. Because the unwanted behavior is already a pattern. One which has formed a habit. Habits do not have to pass through the thinking process before being engaged. They just happen.

So the secret is not to start with the impulse that is already set, but rather the child's own thinking process. Which is the only thing strong enough to change the impulse.

**CAUTION**: dealing with the thinking process does not mean giving a lecture on why it is important to behave in class. That is quite irrelevant at the moment because it is obviously not important to Johnny. But a good parent can make it important.

In spite of all the dazzling distractions that our world has to offer today, it often comes as something of a surprise to parents that they can still have so much impact on their children. That's because nature has instilled in children not only the need for parents but an inborn need to please them. By utilizing this natural drive to their advantage, parents can influence their children's behavior, teach them good habits and skills they will need later in life, and give them the sort of "head start" every child deserves. This phenomenon is at the core of every parent/child relationship. It is a "golden key" when it comes to unlocking the doors to the kind of **motivation** that makes changing behavior a challenge instead of a chore.

Here's how to start:

# ✔ CHECKLIST

✔ Choose an appealing reward. You know your child and the things or activities that are most appealing. It doesn't have to be something purchased. Children are always enthusiastic about activities, especially if it includes some "one-on-one" time.

✔ Make a reachable goal. For example, if Johnny's first session of the day is math, send a note to be signed by the teacher if he can successfully make it through the lesson without being disruptive (approximately half an hour). Don't go "note crazy" and start dividing the day up into half-hour increments. Remember, we're starting small. We are dealing with one session, for one time period only.

✔ Do not be negative if the goal is not reached first day. Now is the time for a discussion but not on the importance of listening in class. The topic should be an acknowledgment of the difficulty of that task, and ideas on how he might succeed tomorrow. For instance, if sitting next to a best friend is making it impossible for Johnny not to talk during the math lesson, he might try requesting to sit somewhere else for that half hour. Not "for good," though. The thought of not sitting next to a best friend forever is too much of a shock. But a half hour (in his mind) he maybe could handle.

✔ Never take an earned reward away. If Johnny did wonders in math that first day but behaved totally outrageous in the afternoon science lesson, think of some other way to handle it that has nothing to do with the reward he already earned. And give it gladly. To "make a deal" and then not follow through for any reason will lower the respect your child has for you. **If you say it, do it.**

✔ Don't quit too soon. Remember, **it takes two weeks to create a habit**. The goal should be to make it through two weeks without fail. If a day or two goes by when he doesn't make it through, you start over. When he successfully completes the two weeks, you can then relegate behavior in math class to "Phase Two" of the reward program.

✔ Don't overload the circuits. The temptation to add another session or behavior pattern to work on grows stronger the closer Johnny gets to his goal. But don't do it. Added pressures and unexpected failures at this time tend to be taken very personally and have repercussions in the self-image department. While Johnny is working on his goal, the major goal of his parents must be to **make sure he succeeds**.

✔ Show your encouragement. Lavish on the praise when he succeeds. Avoid phrases like, "That's how you should have been acting in the first place." And never begrudge the reward. If you made a bargain to stop at the local mini-mart for a treat every day he succeeds, or play a half hour of his favorite game before bed... do it with enthusiasm. Even if you're sick and tired of whatever it is, or hadn't realized how it would break into the time you normally spend doing something else. Stay positive that he is successfully changing his behavior. Realize that if it's been an effort or drudgery for you, it has been equally – or more so – for him.

The secret to being successful with "Phase One" of changing behavior is to **start small, give frequent attainable rewards, and to be consistent enough to form new habits.** The time it takes to form good habits is time well spent, even when starting out small. Once the training process shifts over into habit, it never has to be "relearned" again. It then frees up the thinking process for going on to other things.

Like Phase Two.

> *Increase the value of a desired behavior by increasing the reward.*

## Chapter Six
# Phase Two

The goal of any reward system is to ultimately be replaced by a desired behavior. It is a law of nature. Even though it is human nature that we are discussing here, it is a natural law, none-the-less, and, therefore, indisputable. The human psyche works in this way, and—like many of the other principles we have talked about—works both negatively and positively. Like electricity. One of the most vivid examples of this is the drug dealer who gives out the first of his merchandise for free. Then, for a minimal fee. Then for any high price he he wants. Why does this work so well?

Because the desired behavior has already become a habit.

Behavior, no matter how "ingrained," can be counteracted by a reward that is equal to—or above—its value. And if it is true that only a child's own desire can change a behavior, it is also true that parents hold the power over their children to change their desires. In the example of Johnny not being able to listen in class, we can change that behavior by starting small, making achievable goals, and being consistent. Remember, there is only one goal for Phase One: a successful two-week run of the desired behavior.

At this point, many parents think the job is done and go to work in another problem spot without ever having gone on to Phase Two. Consequently, when the original unwanted behavior pops up again (seemingly out of nowhere), it is extremely frustrating for both parent and child. One rarely goes back to the original reward routine for correcting it, simply because everyone thinks they tried that already, and it obviously didn't work.

But that is the very time when it is most important to go back because your foundation for change is already laid. It will not only be easier this time, it will be twice as powerful. Why? Because while you were busy working with the physical problem of Johnny not listening in class, something was subconsciously changing in his thinking process that will make the changes easier next time. What's more, it will help with many more behaviors than just listening in class.

Phase One is limited. It has merely succeeded in raising a wall, but without reinforcements, even a beautiful wall can only stand up to so much pressure. The same is true of human behavior. We are building a unique (and hopefully wonderful) human being as we raise our children. Like any other piece of construction that have to withstand the elements of life, they must be built strong enough to stand up to whatever purpose they choose to engage in along the way.

Since it is human nature to delegate what is already mastered to that part of the brain which "takes no thought" to the hows and whys anymore, it should come as no surprise that the child will lose interest in what is no longer a challenge. But if the desired behavior is not "set in cement," what do you do?

It's time to up the ante.

Like the drug dealer who begins with only a small fee, you increase the value of the desired behavior by increasing the reward. With one small catch; this time it takes a little longer than a day to earn it. It takes a week. Before Phase One, that request would have been unbelievable for the child. He might not have even given it a try. But he has already done successfully what you are asking him to do. He has done more than a week, he has actually made it through two. He knows it is possible but the big question is, does he want to? That's why it's time to change the reward.

And don't give in to the temptation to cheat here. Children are not dumbbells. The promise of a fantastic vacation when you had every intention of taking one anyway, is not fair. The child is putting forth tremendous effort—even if you think this kind of behavior should come through some kind of osmosis and he should do it naturally. He is setting up patterns for life, and it is your opinion of the value of these patterns that will determine his. If the only reason you are doing all this is to avoid another embarrassing confrontation with the school, then...

Don't worry. Stick to the steps and it will work for you anyway. What's more, your child will get a lot more out of it than you will, in the long run.

Following are the steps for Phase Two.

## ✔ CHECKLIST

✔ **Stay ahead of your child** with the program. Don't wait

until he becomes bored with the daily routine (or the rewards) to change over to Phase Two. The first time he makes it through a successful two weeks, kick things into high gear and keep him charged. For instance, if you have given him fifty cents a day for a reward, tell him how impressed you are with his achievement and that it was worth every penny to you. So much so, that you would even be willing to give him, say... FIVE DOLLARS on Saturday, instead of fifty cents every day.

✔ **Stay age appropriate**. For the sake of example we have been using Johnny, who is having problems listening in grade school. If you have a high school student who is having the same problem, an activity with a parent after school or fifty cents a day is not going to cut it. Longer phone privileges or time with friends is a more valuable reward for an older child.

✔ **Don't be discouraged** if it takes longer than you think to get to Phase Two. All **behavior takes practice**. Chances are, it took a lot more than a few weeks for the unwanted habits to develop in the first place.

✔ **Be consistent**. Once again, consistency is your best ally in changing behavior. While you are busy with your program, the mere repetition of it is busy reinforcing the pattern in the child's subconscious. And if you think you've seen this tip crop up on more than one of these lists, you're right. For obvious reasons.

✔ **Be patient**. Almost everything of value in life takes time and the time you invest in your children will pay far better dividends than the "pastimes" you traded them for.

✔ **Stay reasonable**. Don't go overboard with the rewards. Put some time and thought into what you will agree to before you commit... because your honor is on the line.

Phase Two of changing behavior is an often overlooked step in the reward system. Yet, in the same way that "setting the hook" is a reasonable guarantee that your fish won't get away, stretching out the time span between rewards takes a surface relationship with a behavior to a deeper level. It turns it into a habit. And good habits make children behave better. Which in turn makes happier parents. Now the question is, "What next?" Is there a Phase Three?

You bet.

> Points will work for everyone.

## Chapter Seven
# Phase Three

Rewards are the most efficient system for changing behavior. In Phase One we saw how the rewards needed to be frequent and equal to the value of effort necessary to make a change. In Phase Two we saw the necessity of lengthening the time between those rewards, and maintaining interest levels by raising reward values during that time.

But as we mentioned before, the ultimate goal of any reward system is to produce a desired behavior that will carry on indefinitely without the rewards. Remember, we are shooting for self-discipline, here. So, even while we are proceeding along quite nicely in our desired goals at this point, we are still in a temporary position.

Phase Three takes the final step of exchanging rewards for reinforcements. To do this, we begin by finding a suitable medium of exchange. At this point, you should have a few things already in place that have been "subconsciously" at work for you. The first is **praise**.

If you have been lavishing on the praise at every opportunity, your approval rating should have increased sufficiently in your child's eyes to hold some "swaying power" of its own by now. You can measure this power by the response your child has to your words of encouragement. Does their face "light up?" Do they suddenly strive even harder to please you? Do you see them imitating your praise techniques to siblings or friends as a part of their own interaction with others?

If not, you either haven't been frequent enough with your praise, or you haven't been demonstrative enough. Simply make an adjustment to your deliveries and your children will respond in the above ways. Guaranteed.

Because it is human nature.

If it doesn't happen instantly, it's only because it is out of character for you and will take a little time for your child to believe that such communication is really happening between you. If you're "just not the praising type"... then change your type. Changing behavior works for adults as well as children, and this kind of communication between parent and child offers "rewards" that go way beyond childhood.

The second thing working for you is the child's own success in the thing you are asking him to do. By the time you reach Phase Three there should no longer be any question in the child's mind whether or not he is capable of achieving this goal. At this point, he has already done it. That isn't to say the behavior is "written in stone" just yet, but the cement is definitely drying. Both you and the child have discovered that the behavior is sustainable.

But for how long?

And in the child's eyes, "what's the point?"

Now is the time to introduce the powerhouse of changing behavior... **the point system**. Points work for everybody. In the real world, as well as the world of childhood. Points are the next best medium of exchange to money. If you find this hard to believe, just look at the stock exchange, the measurement for bank loans, or insurance tables. Points—in their many forms—are a necessary part of modern day living. When your child graduates to a point system for desired behavior, he is already taking a vital step into the real world. He's forming good life habits… which make life good.

When it comes to point systems, age doesn't matter. If you have a toddler that is learning to share, points will work. If you have a teenager who wants driving time in the family car, points will work. If you have a child who spends way too much time on video games instead of interacting with others, points will work. The only difference between all of these scenarios is the trade-in value the points stand for. Customize them to your own family needs and values. Once again, consistency is the main key. For constant behavior, you need constant reinforcements.

That doesn't mean you have to forever be rewarding Johnny for listening in class, from the third grade (when you began) until high school graduation. It simply means you have to get him in the habit of exchange. That's the purpose of Phase Three. When we successfully exchange rewards for points, then we can successfully exchange the rewards and reinforcements for other behaviors. Move on to something else you want to work on. That's changing behavior in a nutshell. That's using the secrets of human nature to achieve your success.

So, let's look a little closer at point systems. Here are the necessary ingredients:

# ✔ CHECKLIST

✔ The younger the child, the more visual the system needs to be. Colorful charts, stickers, and animated praise from parents works best with the little ones. Put the chart on the refrigerator (or some other visual location). Use colored markers, drawings, and — if you're not artistic — there are numerous commercial items like this already out there in the marketplace. Charts for household chores and bedtime habits like brushing teeth, etc. The point is to **put up something tangible.**

✔ Make points redeemable at specific times. One of the most common pitfalls of the point system is to let it dwindle away during the business of daily living and suddenly it's been weeks since you've had a "redemption session." **Set a certain time for redeeming those points**. No longer than once a week for younger children. The older ones can go a bit longer for something more valuable, such as a special dress for the prom, or a coveted event that's coming up. But make sure these occasions are never overlooked, or it is your reputation that will suffer.

✔ **Each point must have a specific value**. If ten points is worth an ice cream at the local ice cream shop on one week, it can't be exchanged without notice (and agreement from both parties) to a dish out of the freezer of whatever is left in there. **No substitutes without going back to the bargaining table**.

✔ **Never take points away**. Your paycheck might be "all spent" when you finally get it. but you'd get pretty disgusted if an employer took money out of it for something you didn't do right last week. Kids are the same way. Points earned are points earned. They're sacred. Never take them back for bad behavior, even if you have a junior *Machiavellian* on you hands. There are other ways to deal with unacceptable behavior.

✔ **Do not take achievements lightly**. Never make light of something your child has put a tremendous amount of effort into. Just because you assume everyone should be able to wake up enough to use the bathroom at night, don't belittle your child's efforts (or failures) to do so. Always remember that—whether it's verbalized or not—it is your approval that is ultimately the most important reason for your child's desire to work towards anything. That's a big responsibility.

✔ **Don't let interest lag**. If success doesn't happen fast enough, or if it comes too fast, readjust the system. The best point systems need to stay fine-tuned to the specific needs of the child.

Remember that changing behavior is a family project: you're all on the same side. So, **help your children win**. If you know from experience that Sally can't concentrate on much of anything after eight o'clock, that's no time to schedule a family conference to discuss point values. In the same way, if Jimmy has been trying unsuccessfully for three days not to have physical confrontations with his brother, you need to readjust the time periods and point values so that they reflect a greater incentive for him to try harder. Similarly, if the learned behavior has become common place or too easy, it's time to go on to the next phase. Or the next challenge.

Also try to remember that young children are "concrete": they need to see it, feel it, and touch it. Try using some animated praise. And just what is animated praise? Instead of saying, "Good job, Jennifer, Dad's proud of you," you say, "Way to go, Jenny!" (raised voice, big smile, here. Clap, hug, even jump up and down if you can find it in your psyche to do so. If not, give it your best shot). Remember, it isn't praise unless the child knows it is.

Changing behavior is at the same time both simple and complex. Half the secret of success is to understand the reasons for the behavior in the first place. The truth is, there is no easy solution to any behavioral problem. Understanding human nature and utilizing the forces that are already in motion in the psyche of a child, simply makes it easier. It still takes a tremendous amount of effort on not only your part as a parent, but on your child's part as a child. All children go through phases. Wouldn't it be nice to have more of a say in which ones they went through?

You can.

> *As a parent you are not Fate.*

## Chapter Eight
## **Let The House Rule**

If one of the main goals in changing behavior is to teach children how to discipline themselves, then the consistent application of the programs that are outlined in this book will make a noticeable difference in your home. Each of the suggestions comes with a guarantee for anyone who will take the time and effort to give them a try. How can I make that claim? Because they are based on human nature, which means you only have to be human to qualify. So, if you are reading this book, you most probably are.

But there is one last principle to make note of here.

Even in this age of permissiveness there are some rules that parents will never change their minds about. Toddlers who want to play in the street, preschoolers who insist on staying up after midnight, or ten-year-olds who demand to live on sweets until they are fifteen; have little or no chance at winning when they bring these kind of requests up before a fairly normal parent. Yet, it is not uncommon to see out-and-out battles over these things in public places. No doubt, because the only thing children have going for them in these situations is a parent's reluctance to make a public spectacle of themselves.

So, why does it happen over and over? Because two of the strongest influences on human nature are at work. **Impulse** and **temptation**. Conflicts with these two things run from the beginning of life to the end of it and maturity is often judged by how well a person has gained control over them. Some people never do. Some very gifted people, who–by all indications–should be wildly successful at something, actually miss the mark of their destinies because of their inabilities to cope with these things.

History proves that successful people spring from all walks of life. It makes no difference if one is rich or poor, male or female, or even from one culture or another. But the thing that all successful people do have in common is that they have learned to control impulse and temptation. Some families have been able to hand the keys to their success down to their children, but even this is no guarantee that the heir will be able to drive the thing home. Because, in the end, success is an individual thing and we are all required to make the journey ourselves, no matter how much advice we get.

The secret to dealing successfully with these situations, then, is not to correct your children for the impulses and temptations they have, but to **allow them to experience the consequences for the choices that they make** when faced with them. This produces "**response-ability**." The more opportunities a child has to respond to something, the quicker they will learn the best way to handle it.

If it is true that what a person learns in childhood stays with them all their life, and that at no other time will a person learn as quickly or absorb so much, then maybe the most important of life's lessons should be dealt with in childhood. Children should be given every opportunity to taste and handle impulse and temptation, to make their own decisions, and to realize the consequences of their own choices.

Does this mean you should suffer through an agonizing month of letting that ten-year-old eat nothing but junk and hope that his own natural functions will eventually make him crave vegetables and salads once in awhile? Not at all. Life's consequences are final, and there are many things which would produce devastating effects in our children's future if we were to loose their ignorance and vulnerability out in it too soon. But like the astronaut who has flown countless simulated space missions before he actually "blasts off," parents can begin training their children for the race long before they ever enter it.

This takes some role-playing.

Let's look first at the role of the parent. As a parent, you are not Fate. It is not your duty to decide what your children will do and then force or coerce them into doing it. Nor is it your place to pit yourself against them as a sparring partner, in order for them to learn better how to "deal with things" in life.

You are the wise counselor—the advocate—who is ever on their side through this great trial, and always available for advice when they need it. You are not the judge, for then you would have to be impartial, and it goes against human nature to be impartial with one's own children. Besides that, **the greatest influence over a child is a parent**, (and vice-versa) which makes an automatic conflict whenever these two things are placed opposite of each other. So, the trick is to avoid getting into that position.

Now, let's switch our attention to the child. The most important thing to remember about the child's role in this scenario is that–to them–this is not a game. It is real. To quote a famous source, children "... *believe all things, hope all things, and endure all things.*" They are at the same time vulnerable and resilient. To have the greatest impact during the teachable moments you will be encountering during these simulations, you must remember to–at all times– **treat them with the utmost respect as a person.**

In the same way that most children are born with healthy hearts, lungs, and other vital organs which are fully functional at birth, they also–contrary to popular opinion–come equipped with fully developed sensitivities toward emotions. To insult or criticize them personally for their decisions will undermine not only your efforts to train them, but your relationships with them, as well.

In life there are certain things an individual has no control over. Such as death and taxes, and many other things our society has set down as requirements for peaceful living. Whether or not a person believes in these things has no bearing on them. They are nonnegotiable. We abide by the rules, or we pay the fines. Everything seems to cost, and fairness is not an issue here. That's life. And if it is our goal to model our disciplines to best train up our children for life, then the best family training situation is to have **house rules.**

The rules of the house are non-negotiable in the same way that life is. So, the consequences for breaking them should be made very clear. In this way, the responsibility stays with the child to make the right decisions and to grapple with the consequences himself, if he chooses wrong. Because parents have given the authority of these rules over to the house, they are not in a position to pardon an offense or change the rules with each new situation.

In this way, they can remain sympathetic to their children during these times without giving anger or resentment the ability to block relationships. It is much more difficult for a child to project their displeasure toward a parent who had nothing to do with his decision in the first place. Nine times out of ten, they will seek the parent's solace, or assistance for a way out. And if they do…

Give them one. But make it an acceptable solution—or better yet—two or three options the child can choose from. It is not the purpose of house rules to create the prison mentality of crime and punishment. It is to teach children to successfully deal with their problems. In order to do that, you have to **set them up to succeed.**

For instance, if Johnny ventured into a friend's house whose parents were not home, and it is a house rule that there must always be adult supervision in order to play inside, Mom does not have to take it as a personal challenge to her authority in order to deal with it. She can even express sympathy that he must now choose one of the consequences (that he knows beforehand, so there is no power-struggle for a lesser sentence) that the house rule requires. These might include a restriction of playing with that friend for a specified time, several house chores as penance; early bedtime, or whatever else you and your children have agreed upon as an appropriate consequence when the house rule was made.

Once the "fine" has been paid, let it be paid in full. If you agreed that this was an appropriate consequence before it actually happened, it is unfair and unethical for you to show anger or disappointment after the child has "paid his dues." Nagging about it after the fact will cause a lack of respect for you, not the rule, as well as a lack of self-confidence in the child when it comes to making decisions. Remember, the most important thing for the child is your relationship. If there is a rift in that, all learning stops until it is resolved.

House rules can relieve a lot of the everyday tensions and disagreements that confront families and rob them of quality time together. By delegating the burden of your non-negotiable rules to the house, you can have more time and energy for meaningful communications over issues that really matter. The proper use of house rules strengthens relationships and establishes and affirms family values. Children are more secure if they know what is expected of them, and more independent if they are allowed to make choices.

Following are some guidelines for setting up House Rules that will help you in establishing your own.

# ✔ CHECKLIST

- ✔ **House rules are non-negotiable**. Bedtimes do not come under this category because they change with the interruptions of daily schedules and with the ages of individual children. On the other hand, behavior at bedtime can be incorporated into a house rule (if this is a problem area for you) because you can decide beforehand what the desired behavior is, and what the consequences will be if it is not followed.

- ✔ **Let your children participate in setting down the rules and consequences.** That way they will carry more weight and leave less room for argument later because they helped to establish them. Arguments are easily quelled with "We made that a house rule, remember? We don't change those."

- ✔ **Don't change the rules**. If you agreed to the consequences when the rules were set down, you should never add anything to them because you were "really upset about it" when it actually happened. **Consistency is the strongest form of discipline there is**, not anger.

- ✔ **Don't make too many.** Too many rules can bog anybody down so try to stick to the ones that are most important to you. Pick and choose the problem areas you want to deal with, and don't set yourself up to be the perfect family overnight. Remember practice makes perfect and the only way to get there is to endure the mistakes and mishaps along the way.

- ✔ **Stick to your rules**. If you don't get into the habit of enforcing the house rules and slip back into bickering over every incident, again... they won't be much help to you.

✔ **Provide     choices     when     setting     down consequences.** This lets the debate rest with which choice the child will make for his infraction as opposed to protesting against having any consequence at all. A simple "Shall you choose, or should I?" almost always results in cooperation, simply because a disagreeable choice is better than no choice at all.

House rules are another way to help turn your family time into prime time. They are the final step in continuing your programs for teaching your children to discipline themselves, without having to take every moment of your free time to do it. What's more, it takes the burden off you and your children in those moments that should be spent enjoying instead of challenging each other. So, the next time your children get into a royal battle while you're making dinner and it takes fifteen minutes to settle who started it… don't. Make it a house rule that fighting brings a consequence to both participants.

Then let the house rule.

# THE HELP

On the next few pages are three examples of progress tracking for children that are age-oriented. A point game for the very young, a weekly point sheet for intermediate ages, and a contract for teenagers. All of these are simply to give you help with ideas, and you may modify any or all of them for your own use.

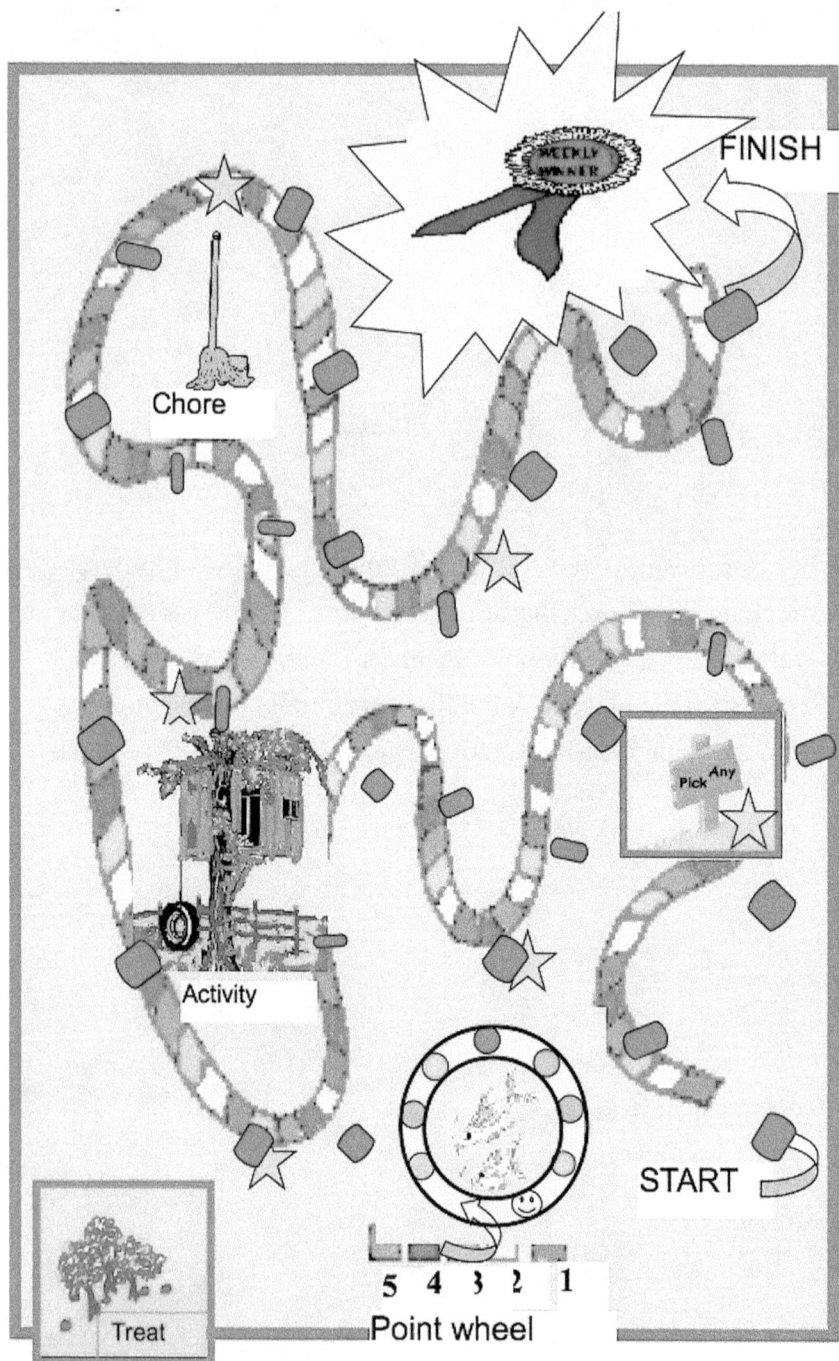

FINISH

WEEKLY WINNER

Chore

Pick Any

Activity

START

Treat

5  4  3  2  1
Point wheel

68

## THE POINT GAME

For younger children, it works better to have something more visual than just writing down numbers, or keeping a tally for points on a post-it note on the refrigerator. The example is something that can be modified to your own needs (such as point values and specific behaviors or chores you are working on). It can also be simplified for the very young by using a magnet (for playing on the refrigerator) on the larger "rainbow" squares, so that the game won't be so long they lose interest. This way, the game can be completed in a day, or a week, or anywhere in between.

The point wheel allows for "side trips" worth an early reward for those who might choose that option when landing on a star. However, the playing piece usually begins in the same place on the "rainbow road" when they return. The point boxes beneath the wheel may be assigned for specific activities, projects, or chores. Older children might simply want to keep track of their progress by coloring in squares with a marker or colored pencil.

**IMPORTANT REMINDER**: Never take points away! A child might be stuck in the same place for a long time until he/ she earns more points, but they must never lose what they have already earned. In the same way, any treats or activities you have assigned to the game should not be obtainable in any other way but by participation in the game. The strength of THE POINT GAME depends on these two things.

The illustration gives a general example that you may change and adjust to suit your family's particular preferences. Use a pair of dice to move around the point wheel, make a spinner, or simply assign values to the colors. If you're the creative type, you can start from scratch and make your own game up. It's up to you.

## Weekly Point Sheet

| Chores and Projects | Monday | Tuesday | Wednesday | Thursday | Friday | Saturday | Sunday |
|---|---|---|---|---|---|---|---|
| | | | | | | | |
| | | | | | | | |
| | | | | | | | |
| | | | | | | | |
| | | | | | | | |
| **Rewards** | | | | | | | |
| | | | | | | | |
| | | | | | | | |
| | | | | | | | |
| **Bonus Points** | | | | | | | |
| | | | | | | | |
| | | | | | | | |

**Weekly Goal** _____ **Bonus Points**_____

WEEKLY POINT SHEET

Older children tend to enjoy keeping track of their own points and having parents (or other caregivers) initial the boxes when a behavior or chore is approved. The strength of this system lies in–once again–never taking points away, and by deciding on specific goals beforehand. For example: thirty-five points might be the goal for the weekly reward, but there are opportunities to make many more. Use bonus rewards (decide what these might be beforehand) for points that are made beyond the goal. In this way, children become accustomed to moving on to another goal when one is reached, as opposed to backing off on their efforts after the first goal is met.

**Tip for success:** If your child never makes it to the bonus goal, lower the requirements accordingly so that the goals remain achievable.

## CONTRACT

Teenagers need to be held accountable in ways that are as close to the real world as possible. That's why it becomes important that their word be their bond in the same way that it is for adults. A written contract such as the sample provided

---

**AGREEMENT OF SERVICES**

This Agreement is to serve as a contract between _____

and _____ for the purpose of exchanging services for privileges and

expenses from the period of _____ to _____ .

I _____ residing at _____

do hereby agree to perform the following services:

_____

_____

_____

_____

_____

In exchange for the following privileges:

_____

_____

_____

_____

_____

Expenses included for this period:      Yes _____  No _____

If yes, these expenses shall include the sum of _____

Agreed upon this day of _____ to last until the date of _____
Or until both parties shall jointly agree and draw up another or modified agreement.

Signed:

(Teen)                                        Parent(s)

_____                    _____

_____

---

works well to remind both parties what they have agreed on and signed their name to.

This form of agreement also makes settlements easier, and should be handled just as they are in society. Did you agree to these things? Did you perform them? Then you are (or aren't) entitled to the provisions of the agreement. Once again, do not take away privileges already earned, and be reasonable during negotiations beforehand.

**Reminder:** The more you treat a teen like an adult, the more they will act like one.

## EXPLANATION OF AGREEMENT

This Agreement is made to serve as a contract between (your name) and (child's name)

For the purpose of exchanging services for privileges and expenses from the period of (date) to (date).

I (child's name) residing at (home address) do hereby agree to perform the following services:

(list of services)

In exchange for the following privileges:

(list of privileges)

Expenses included for this period: (list here, if any)

If yes, these expenses shall include the sum of (amount)

Agreed upon this day of (date) to last until (date). Or, until both parties shall jointly agree and draw up a modified agreement.

Signed: (signature of child)

Signed: (signature of parents)

Teaching children to discipline themselves by making them responsible for their own behavior not only makes parenting easier, but better prepares them for life. It also goes a long way toward helping them feel more secure and self-confident in our rapidly changing world. Using this program – in whole, or in part – will help you do that.

Happy parenting!

*Attention is respect... no matter how old you are.*

*"Train up a child in the way that he should go: and when he is old, he will not depart from it."*

*Proverbs 22:6 KJV*

Other books by
# Lilly Maytree

*Novels:*
Gold Trap
The Pandora Box

*The Stella Madison Capers:*
Home Before Dark
A Thief In The House
Sea Trials
The Pushover Plot
Lost In The Wilderness
The Last Resort
Voyage of the Dreadnaught

*For Writers:*
Unspoken Rules

*For Parents:*
Behave Yourself!
*Teaching children to dicipline themselves.*

The Nature of Children
(And how to deal with it.)

# About the Author

As a former educator, and co-founder of the Wilderness School Institute, Lilly Maytree has developed curriculum for outdoor activities that incorporate nature studies, wilderness skills, and motivational behavior programs. Many of which were for troubled youth through state agencies.

After years of experience, she has a lot to say about what motivates children, and has implemented many of those unique ideas into books and programs that others can use. She is also the author of: ***The Nature of Children (and how to deal with it)***, a handbook for parenting tots to teens. You can get in touch with her by visiting:

LillyMaytree.com

Thank you for purchasing this book sponsored by the Wilderness School Institute. Your support helps us to maintain the website and continue to offer high-quality resources to families everywhere. If you found *Behave Yourself!* helpful, please let us know! You can share your opinions and experiences about it over at:

**WildernessSchoolInstitute.org**

You can also find helpful articles and tips about dealing with children over at:

**SummersIslandPress.com**

Simply click through to the "For Parents" tab when you get there. You might also enjoy takiing a few moments to browse through the many books and activities for children based on the methods we have talked about here.